Exquisite Delights: Indulge in the Creamy Aromas

Discover Authentic Thai Cuisine with Creamy Sensations

By Mary Thompson

Mary Thompson

© Copyright 2023 by Mary Thompson - All rights reserved.

This document is geared towards providing exact and reliable information in regard to the topic and issue covered. The publication is sold with the idea that the publisher is not required to render accounting, officially permitted, or otherwise, qualified services. If advice is necessary, legal or professional, a practiced individual in the profession should be ordered.

From a Declaration of Principles which was accepted and approved equally by a Committee of the American Bar Association and a Committee of Publishers and Associations.

In no way is it legal to reproduce, duplicate, or transmit any part of this document in either electronic means or in printed format. Recording of this publication is strictly prohibited and any storage of this document is not allowed unless with written permission from the publisher. All rights reserved.

The information provided herein is stated to be truthful and consistent, in that any liability, in terms of inattention or otherwise, by any usage or abuse of any policies, processes, or directions contained within is the solitary and utter responsibility of the recipient reader. Under no circumstances will any legal responsibility or blame be held against the publisher for any reparation, damages, or monetary loss due to the information herein, either directly or indirectly.

Respective authors own all copyrights not held by the publisher.

The information herein is offered for informational purposes solely and is universal as so. The presentation of the information is without contract or any type of guarantee assurance.

The trademarks that are used are without any consent, and the publication of the trademark is without permission or backing by the trademark owner. All trademarks and brands within this book are for clarifying purposes only and are owned by the owners themselves, not affiliated with this document.

Table of contents

Introduction 1

Chapter 1: Thai Snack Recipes 3

- 1.1 Thai Veggie Burger Recipe 3
- 1.2 Thai Style Popcorn Recipe 4
- 1.3 Sticky Thai Meatballs Recipe 6
- 1.4 Leaf Wrapped Snack Recipe 7
- 1.5 Thai Pork Snack Recipe 8
- 1.6 Thai Shrimp Appetizers Recipe 9
- 1.7 Thai Fries Recipe 10
- 1.8 Thai Style Salsa Recipe 12
- 1.9 Thai Toast Recipe 13
- 1.10 Thai Shrimp Cake Recipe 15
- 1.11 Thai Pork Toast Recipe 16
- 1.12 Thai Granola Recipe 18
- 1.13 Thai Pineapple Snack Recipe 20
- 1.14 Thai Fried Peanuts Recipe 21
- 1.15 Thai Fish Cakes Recipe 22
- 1.16 Thai Sweet Potato Skins Recipe 23

Chapter 2: Thai Breakfast Recipes 25

- ❖ 2.1 Thai Breakfast Omelet Recipe 25
- ❖ 2.2 Yam Kai (Thai Eggs) with Leftover Grains Recipe 28
- ❖ 2.3 Thai Breakfast Rice Soup with Shrimp Recipe 30
- ❖ 2.4 Thai French Toast Recipe 32
- ❖ 2.5 Thai Breakfast Quesadilla Recipe 34
- ❖ 2.6 Thai Breakfast Bowl Recipe 36
- ❖ 2.7 Thai Breakfast Bake Recipe 38
- ❖ 2.8 Thai Breakfast Baskets Recipe 40

Chapter 3: Thai Lunch Recipes 42

- ❖ 3.1 Pad Thai Recipe 42
- ❖ 3.2 Easy Thai Noodles Recipes 44
- ❖ 3.3 Thai Red Curry Recipe 46
- ❖ 3.4 Thai Som Tum without Papaya Recipe 48
- ❖ 3.5 Hot and Sour Noodle Soup with Prawns Recipe 50
- ❖ 3.6 Thai Chicken Salad Recipe 52
- ❖ 3.7 Quick Thai Salad Recipe 54
- ❖ 3.8 Thai Chopped Salad with Sesame Garlic Dressing Recipe 56
- ❖ 3.9 Beef Pad Thai Recipe 58
- ❖ 3.10 Pork Pad Thai Recipe 60
- ❖ 3.11 Thai Fish Curry Recipe 62
- ❖ 3.12 Thai Basil Chicken Recipe 64

- ❖ 3.13 Thai Crunch Salad with Peanut Butter Dressing Recipe 66
- ❖ 3.14 Thai Chicken Coconut Curry Recipe 68
- ❖ 3.15 Thai Green Curry Soup Recipe 70
- ❖ 3.16 Thai Rice Noodles with Chicken and Asparagus Recipe................. 72
- ❖ 3.17 Thai Chicken Fried Rice Recipe 74

Chapter 4: Thai Dinner Recipes 76

- ❖ 4.1 Thai Slow Cooker Chicken Curry Recipe 76
- ❖ 4.2 Thai Slow Cooker Whole Cauliflower Curry Recipe...................... 78
- ❖ 4.3 Thai Slow Cooker Chicken Carrot Potato Soup Recipe 80
- ❖ 4.4 Thai Slow Cooker Coconut Quinoa Curry Recipe 81
- ❖ 4.5 Thai Slow Cooker Eggplant Curry Recipe....................................... 82
- ❖ 4.6 Thai Slow Cooker Yellow Curry Recipe 84
- ❖ 4.7 Thai Slow Cooker Vegetable Massaman Curry Recipe 85
- ❖ 4.8 Thai Pumpkin and Veggie Curry Recipe 87
- ❖ 4.9 Thai Vegan Drunken Noodles Recipe 89
- ❖ 4.10 Thai Tofu Green Curry with Quinoa Recipe 90

Conclusion 92

Introduction

Thailand is the most acclaimed country in the entire world for its cooking. Navigating from the southern landmass toward the northern areas, the country offers a different blend of frantically tasty food. The south of Thailand is acclaimed for its red-hot curries, profound usage of coconut milk, and astounding fish plans.

The northeastern part is remarkable for its vegetables filled plates of blended greens and flavors, grilled meat, sausages, and tenacious rice. Bangkok, the greatest city, attracts Thais from all around the country to make a perpetual mix of alluring flavors to taste.

From streak cooked sautés to hand beaten servings of mixed greens, if you appreciate eating, you will be in heaven with the assortment and amount of food in this cuisine given in this book. You will get over 77 different breakfast, lunch, dinner, and snack recipes that you can easily start cooking at home with the detailed instructions present below each recipe.

Preparing your easy Thai food at home without the need to order food from some restaurant can become very easy once you start reading this book. So, why wait for more? Let us dive deep into the world of Thai cuisine.

Chapter 1: Thai Snack Recipes

This Chapter contains those easy Thai snack recipes that you have been longing to make in your kitchen.

❖ 1.1 Thai Veggie Burger Recipe

Cooking Time: 10 minutes
Serving Size: 4

Ingredients:

- Thai red curry paste, two tbsp.
- Salt, a pinch
- Mix vegetables, two cups
- Thai red curry paste, four tbsp.
- Vegetable oil, two tbsp.
- Green onions, half cup
- Cilantro, half cup
- Garlic and ginger paste, one tsp.
- Thai pickles, as required
- Bread buns, four

Instructions:

1. Mix all the stuff for the burger mixture together and make patty.

2. Fry the patties and then assemble the patty burger by adding pickles into it.
3. Your burger is ready to be served.

❖ 1.2 Thai Style Popcorn Recipe

Cooking Time: 10 minutes
Serving Size: 4

Ingredients:
- Thai popcorn sauce, as required
- Popcorn kernels, half cup
- Oil, three tbsp.

Instructions:
1. In a large pot on medium to medium-low heat, add oil and un-popped popcorn kernels.
2. Stir until all the kernels are coated in oil.
3. Cover the pot with a lid.
4. Remove the pot from heat when the frequency of pops reduces.
5. Mix and serve.

❖ 1.3 Sticky Thai Meatballs Recipe

Cooking Time: 20 minutes

Serving Size: 4

Ingredients:
- Beef mince, one pound
- Thai sauce, half cup
- Thai mix spice, two tbsp.
- Bread crumbs, half cup
- Egg, one

Instructions:
1. Preheat the oven.
2. Combine all the ingredients for the meatballs except ground beef in a bowl and mix well.
3. Make small meatballs.
4. Bake for twenty minutes till they are cooked through, and slightly brown.
5. Mix them in the sauce.
6. Your dish is ready to be served.

❖ 1.4 Leaf Wrapped Snack Recipe

Cooking Time: 10 minutes

Serving Size: 4

Ingredients:
- Chalpu leaves, four
- Thai chilies, ten
- Roasted peanuts, half cup
- Grated coconut, half cup
- Thai sauce, four tbsp.
- Chopped ginger, two tbsp.
- Dried shrimps, as required

Instructions:
1. Mix all the ingredients together.
2. Place the mixture onto the middle of the leaf and fold properly.
3. Your dish is ready to be served.

❖ 1.5 Thai Pork Snack Recipe

Cooking Time: 10 minutes

Serving Size: 4

Ingredients:

- Oyster sauce, two tbsp.
- Soy sauce, one tbsp.
- Minced pork, half pound
- Eggs, three
- Coriander leaves, as required
- Bread, one loaf

Instructions:

1. Mix seasonings with pork very well with hand.
2. Add in the Thai soy sauce
3. Cut bread and put minced pork mixture on it.
4. Toss it in egg.
5. Fry in vegetable oil.
6. Fry pork side first.
7. Eat with sweet cull sauce with minced cucumber.
8. Your dish is ready to be served.

❖ 1.6 Thai Shrimp Appetizers Recipe

Cooking Time: 10 minutes

Serving Size: 4

Ingredients:
- Green onions, one
- Oil, two tbsp.
- Lime juice, three tbsp.
- Crushed red pepper flakes, two tbsp.
- Cilantro, one tbsp.
- Minced garlic, one tbsp.
- Lime zest, one tsp.
- Salt and pepper, to taste
- Soy sauce, two tbsp.

Instructions:
1. In a large bowl, combine the ingredients.
2. Add the shrimp; turn to coat.
3. Cover and refrigerate for thirty minutes.
4. Drain and discard marinade; arrange shrimp on a serving plate.
5. Your dish is ready to be served.

❖ 1.7 Thai Fries Recipe

Cooking Time: 10 minutes

Serving Size: 4

Ingredients:
- Fries, two pounds
- Fish sauce four tbsp.
- Garlic powder, one tbsp.
- Ground coriander, one tbsp.
- Mix cheese, two cups
- Lime juice, two tbsp.
- Siracha, half cup
- Mayonnaise, half cup
- Green onions, half cup
- Avocado slices, one
- Peanuts, half cup
- Cilantro, as required

Instructions:
1. In a large bowl, toss freshly cooked fries with fish sauce, garlic powder, ground coriander, and salt.

2. Spread half of the cooked, seasoned fries out on a rimmed baking sheet.
3. Cover with half of the cheeses evenly.
4. Top with remaining fries, and then top with the remaining cheeses.
5. Broil on high until the cheese is melted and bubbly, approximately 2 to 3 minutes.
6. In a small bowl, whisk together Sriracha, mayonnaise and lime juice.
7. Top fries with cilantro, peanuts, green onion, avocado and Sriracha mayonnaise. Serve with lime wedges.

❖ 1.8 Thai Style Salsa Recipe

Cooking Time: 10 minutes

Serving Size: 4

Ingredients:

- Chopped grape tomatoes, two cups
- Fresh cilantro, half cup
- Red curry paste, two tbsp.
- Toasted sesame oil, two tbsp.
- Fresh lime juice, two tbsp.
- Salt and pepper, to taste
- Serrano chili, half cup

Instructions:

1. Whisk together fresh lime juice, red curry paste, toasted sesame oil, and kosher salt in a medium bowl.
2. Add chopped grape tomatoes and seeded and minced serrano chili; toss well to combine.
3. Stir in chopped fresh cilantro.
4. Let it stay ten minutes before serving.
5. Your dish is ready to be served.

❖ 1.9 Thai Toast Recipe

Cooking Time: 10 minutes

Serving Size: 4

Ingredients:
- Shrimps, one pound
- Bread slices, eight
- Garlic powder, two tbsp.
- Spring onion, half cup
- Salt and pepper, to taste
- Cilantro, half cup
- Fish sauce, one tsp.
- Soy sauce, one tsp.

Instructions:
1. Add the shrimp to a food processor and turn the shrimp into a paste.
2. Add this to a mixing bowl, along with everything but the oil and bread and mix it really well.
3. Spread the mixture on top of the slices of bread, being generous with the amount on each one.

4. Lay each slice down, meat mixture side down, into the skillet.
5. Cook for a few minutes, being careful not to lift it too early.
6. Cook the Thai toast on the other side, a few more minutes, or until it turns a golden brown.
7. Set the toast on a serving dish.

❖ 1.10 Thai Shrimp Cake Recipe

Cooking Time: 10 minutes

Serving: 2

Ingredients:
- Shrimp, half pound
- All-purpose flour, one cup
- Corn flour, half cup
- Mix Thai spice, one tsp.
- Vegetable oil, for frying
- Egg, one

Instructions:
1. Mix all the dried ingredients together.
2. Add the shrimp into the egg mixture first and then coat it in the dried ingredients.
3. Fry each shrimp.
4. Your dish is ready to be served with you preferred sauce.

❖ 1.11 Thai Pork Toast Recipe

Cooking Time: 10 minutes

Serving Size: 4

Ingredients:
- Pork, one pound
- Bread slices, eight
- Garlic powder, two tbsp.
- Spring onion, half cup
- Salt and pepper, to taste
- Cilantro, half cup
- Fish sauce, one tsp.
- Soy sauce, one tsp.

Instructions:
1. Add the pork to a food processor and turn the pork into a paste.
2. Add this to a mixing bowl, along with everything but the oil and bread and mix it really well.
3. Spread the mixture on top of the slices of bread, being generous with the amount on each one.
4. Lay each slice down, meat mixture side down, into the skillet.

5. Cook for a few minutes, being careful not to lift it too early.
6. Cook the Thai toast on the other side, a few more minutes, or until it turns a golden brown.
7. Set the toast on a serving dish.

❖ 1.12 Thai Granola Recipe

Cooking Time: 31 minutes

Serving: 6

Ingredients:
- Honey, half cup
- Vanilla extract, one tsp.
- Oats, two cups
- Ground flax seeds, half cup
- Pecan, half cup
- Chocolate chips, one cup
- Dried cranberries, one cup
- Brown sugar, one cup
- Vegetable oil, two tbsp.
- Wheat germ, a quarter cup
- Cinnamon, half tsp.
- Salt, to taste

Instructions:
1. Stir brown sugar, honey, vegetable oil, and salt together in a large microwave-safe bowl.

2. Mix oats, cranberries, pecans, ground flax seed, chocolate chips, and wheat germ together in a bowl.
3. Stir vanilla extract and cinnamon into brown sugar mixture.
4. Your dish is ready to be served.

❖ 1.13 Thai Pineapple Snack Recipe

Cooking Time: 5 minutes

Serving: 2

Ingredients:

- Pineapple chunks, one cup
- Vegetable oil, one tbsp.
- Corn, one cup
- Soy sauce, one tbsp.
- Oyster sauce, one tbsp.

Instructions:

1. In a large wok add all the things together.
2. Let it cook for five minutes.
3. Your dish is ready to be served.

❖ 1.14 Thai Fried Peanuts Recipe

Cooking Time: 10 minutes

Serving: 6

Ingredients:
- Sea salt, as required
- Flavored oil, as required
- Peanuts, six ounces

Instructions:
1. Place the peanuts in a strainer or colander, and rinse under water.
2. In a clean wok, add in the air-dried peanuts and enough oil to just cover the peanuts.
3. Then turn on the heat to medium low.
4. Cook for ten minutes.
5. Strain the peanuts out, and spread them out on a baking sheet to cool completely. Sprinkle with salt.
6. Your dish is ready to be served.

❖ 1.15 Thai Fish Cakes Recipe

Cooking Time: 10 minutes

Serving: 2

Ingredients:
- Prawn, half pound
- All-purpose flour, one cup
- Corn flour, half cup
- Mix Thai spice, one tsp.
- Vegetable oil, for frying
- Egg, one

Instructions:
1. Mix all the dried ingredients together.
2. Add the prawns into the egg mixture first and then coat it in the dried ingredients.
3. Fry each prawn.
4. Your dish is ready to be served with you preferred sauce.

❖ 1.16 Thai Sweet Potato Skins Recipe

Cooking Time: 20 minutes

Serving Size: 4

Ingredients:
- Sweet potatoes, one pound
- Spring onions, half cup
- Peanut butter, one cup
- Lime juice, two tbsp.
- Soy sauce, one tbsp.
- Chili, one
- Coconut milk, one cup
- Brown sugar, one tbsp.
- Lemon grass paste, one tsp.

Instructions:
1. Preheat the oven.
2. Place the sweet potatoes in the oven until cooked.
3. Mix the peanut butter, lime juice, soy sauce, chili, coconut milk, brown sugar, ground coriander, spring onions and lemon grass paste until combined.

4. Place the skins on a baking tray and place back in the oven for five minutes to crisp up.
5. Combine the peanut butter sauce mix with the sweet potato filling and mix using a fork.
6. Take the potato skins out of the oven, and fill with the peanut/potato mixture.
7. Place it in the oven.
8. Take out of the oven and place on a plate.

Chapter 2: Thai Breakfast Recipes

Food is tremendously important in Thai culture, with Thais using food as a regular agreeable trade. There are various notable dishes in Thailand and a ton of regional fortes. This Chapter contains those easy Thai breakfast recipes that you have been longing to make in your kitchen.

❖ 2.1 Thai Breakfast Omelet Recipe

Cooking Time: 15 minutes
Serving Size: 2

Ingredients:

- Vegetable oil, one and a half tbsp.
- Sliced mushrooms, one cup
- Eggs, eight
- Sliced red capsicum, one large
- Chopped tomatoes, two medium sized
- Bean sprouts, one cup
- Fresh coriander leaves, half cup
- Fish sauce, one tbsp.
- Lime juice, two tbsp.
- Sliced red chili, one long

- Green beans, one cup

Instructions:
1. Whisk eggs, lime juice, fish sauce, quarter cup water and half of the chili in a large jug.
2. Heat two teaspoons of oil in a medium non-stick frying pan over medium-high heat.
3. Cook mushroom and capsicum, stir, for five minutes or until golden and tender.
4. Add tomato.
5. Cook, stirring, for two minutes or until slightly softened. Meanwhile, place green beans in a heatproof bowl.
6. Cover with boiling water.
7. Wait for few minutes and then drain.
8. Rinse under cold water.
9. Combine mushroom mixture, beans and sprouts in a bowl.
10. Wipe the pan clean.
11. Heat one teaspoon of remaining oil in pan over medium-high heat.
12. Pour quarter of the egg mixture into pan.
13. Swirl to coat.
14. Cook for thirty seconds or until just set.

15. Repeat with remaining oil and egg mixture to make four omelets.
16. Place quarter of the mushroom mixture over one half of each omelet.
17. Fold over to enclose filling.
18. Serve by sprinkling with coriander and remaining chili.

❖ 2.2 Yam Kai (Thai Eggs) with Leftover Grains Recipe

Cooking Time: 10 minutes
Serving Size: 2

Ingredients:

- Vegetable oil, one and a half tbsp.
- Cooked pork chops, one cup
- Eggs, four
- Sliced scallions, four
- Sliced shallots, two medium sized
- Cooked barley, one cup
- Fresh coriander leaves, half cup
- Fish sauce, one tbsp.
- Lime juice, two tbsp.
- Sliced red chili, one long

Instructions:

1. In a medium bowl, stir together the lime juice, fish sauce, one teaspoon of the chili, and the cooked grain of your choice.

2. Put the eggs and the remaining half teaspoon of chili paste in a small bowl and beat with a fork to combine.
3. In a large heavy sauté pan, heat half tablespoon of the oil over medium-high heat.
4. Add the shallots, the white sections of the scallions, the pork, and cook until the shallots are very dark brown and shriveled, for about four minutes.
5. Add the scallion greens and the remaining half tablespoon of oil and cook for one minute.
6. Pour in the egg mixture and cook without disturbing for thirty seconds, then turn and stir, breaking it up a little but keeping good-size pieces together, cooking until just set, about one minute.
7. Pour in the grain mixture and cook, turning with a spatula, until heated through, for about one minute.
8. Your dish is ready to be served.

❖ 2.3 Thai Breakfast Rice Soup with Shrimp Recipe

Cooking Time: 10 minutes

Serving Size: 4

Ingredients:
- Soy sauce, one and a half tbsp.
- Pork stock, three cups
- Jasmine rice, four cups
- Garlic cloves, four
- White peppercorns, one tsp.
- Cilantro, one cup
- Shrimps, 150 grams
- Fish sauce, one tbsp.

Instructions:
1. Pound white peppercorns until fine, then add garlic and cilantro and pound until fine.
2. Add half of this paste to your small pieces of shrimp and mix well.
3. Sauté the small pieces of shrimp in a pan with a little bit of oil just until it is cooked through.

4. Deglaze the pan with some stock as needed and scrape any bits of herb stuck to the bottom.
5. Remove from pan and set aside.
6. If using whole garnish shrimp, sear the whole shrimp over medium high heat until browned and cooked through.
7. Bring the stock to a boil in a pot, add the other half of the herb paste and simmer for one minute.
8. Season with fish sauce and soy sauce, then taste and adjust the seasoning.
9. When ready to serve, bring the broth to a boil then add the rice and the shrimp.
10. Bring the soup back to a simmer, and immediately turn off the heat.
11. Your dish is ready to be served.

❖ 2.4 Thai French Toast Recipe

Cooking Time: 5 minutes

Serving Size: 6

Ingredients:

- Sweetened condensed milk, for garnish
- Eggs, two
- White bread, six slices
- Granulated sugar, two tablespoons
- Whole milk, half cup
- Vegetable oil, half cup
- Kosher salt, a pinch

Instructions:

1. In a medium bowl, whisk together the milk, eggs, sugar, and salt until combined.
2. Pour the mixture into a shallow dish, and then dip each slice of bread into the batter.
3. In a wok, heat the vegetable oil to 325 degrees and line a sheet pan with a wire rack.
4. Working with two slices at a time, and fry, flipping once until golden brown, two minutes per side.
5. Transfer each slice to the prepared sheet pan to drain.

6. Divide the French toast between plates and top each piece with a heavy drizzle of sweetened condensed milk.
7. Your dish is ready to be served.

❖ 2.5 Thai Breakfast Quesadilla Recipe

Cooking Time: 10 minutes

Serving Size: 2

Ingredients:
- Red bell peppers, a quarter cup
- Flour tortillas, two
- Small green onion
- Thai peanut satay sauce, two tablespoons
- Grilled chicken, four ounces
- Reduced fat monetary jack cheese, half cup

Instructions:
1. Heat a skillet over medium-low heat.
2. Place two tortillas on a clean workspace.
3. Top one tortilla with Monterey Jack cheese, sliced chicken, peanut satay sauce, sliced red peppers, and green onions.
4. Place the second tortilla on top of the ingredients.
5. Spray top of the tortilla lightly with nonstick olive oil cooking spray.
6. Transfer quesadilla into preheated skillet.
7. Cook for five minutes, or until golden brown.

8. Spray top tortilla, and then flip in skillet.
9. Cook until golden brown.
10. Your dish is ready to be served.

❖ 2.6 Thai Breakfast Bowl Recipe

Cooking Time: 1 minutes

Serving Size: 6

Ingredients:
- Chopped bell peppers, one
- Minced garlic, one
- Shredded carrots, five
- Toasted cashews, one cup
- Coconut milk, fourteen ounces
- Salt, half tsp.
- Shredded kale leaves, two and a half cups
- Blackberries, one and half cup
- Shredded Napa cabbage, two and a half cups
- Yellow curry powder, one tbsp.
- Ghee, one tsp.
- Garlic chili paste, one tsp.
- Lime juice, one tsp.

Instructions:
1. Place the dressing ingredients into a blender.
2. Blend on high until smooth and creamy throughout.

3. Add salad ingredients to a large bowl and toss with as much dressing as you would like.
4. Add a little bit of it at a time.
5. Your dish is ready to be served.

❖ 2.7 Thai Breakfast Bake Recipe

Cooking Time: 35 minutes

Serving Size: 4

Ingredients:
- Minced garlic, one tsp.
- Minced garlic, one
- Diced tomatoes, one medium
- Grated potatoes, four cups
- Ground cumin, half tsp.
- Salt, half tsp.
- Ground coriander, half tsp.
- Red bell pepper, one small
- Coconut aminos, half tsp.
- Coconut milk, a quarter cup
- Ghee, one tsp.
- Eggs, four
- Lime juice, one tsp.

Instructions:
1. Preheat the oven to 350 degrees.
2. In a cast iron pan, melt the ghee over medium heat.

3. Add the onion, garlic, ginger, and red pepper and sauté until the onion starts to get translucent.
4. Add the coconut milk, coconut aminos, lime juice, spices, sand salt and mix.
5. Cook for another five minutes.
6. Add the tomato and sweet potato and mix well to combine.
7. Turn the stovetop off and transfer the pan to the oven and bake for twenty-five minutes.
8. Remove from the oven, and turn the oven to broil.
9. Make four little wells in the sweet potatoes and crack an egg in each.
10. Place the pan back in the oven on the top rack for five minutes depending on how you like your eggs cooked.
11. Your dish is ready to be served.

❖ 2.8 Thai Breakfast Baskets Recipe

Cooking Time: 20 minutes

Serving Size: 4

Ingredients:
- Minced green onion, one
- Minced jalapeno, a quarter cup
- Egg roll wrappers, eight
- Mango, one small
- Queso fresco, a quarter cup
- Avocado, one small
- Salsa Verde, a quarter cup
- Sesame oil, one tsp.
- Pumpkin seeds, to garnish
- Lime juice, one tsp.

Instructions:
1. Press wraps into nonstick muffin cups.
2. Bake at 375 degrees for seven minutes or till lightly browned and crisp.
3. Remove baskets from cups to wire rack to cool.

4. Combine remaining ingredients in medium sized bowl.
5. Fill each basket, dividing equally.
6. Garnish with pumpkin seeds and serve.

Chapter 3: Thai Lunch Recipes

This Chapter contains those easy Thai lunch recipes that you have been longing to make in your kitchen.

❖ 3.1 Pad Thai Recipe

Cooking Time: 15 minutes
Serving Size: 4

Ingredients:
- Chopped green onions, three
- Eggs, two
- Fresh bean sprouts, half cup
- Garlic cloves, three
- Oil, three tbsp.
- Shrimp or chicken, eight ounces
- Limes, two
- Red bell pepper, one
- Flat rice noodles, eight ounces
- Dry roasted peanuts, two cups
- Soy sauce, one tbsp.
- Light brown sugar, five tbsp.
- Fish sauce, three tbsp.

- Creamy peanut butter, two tbsp.
- Rice vinegar, two tbsp.
- Siracha hot sauce, one tbsp.

Instructions:
1. Cook noodles according to package instructions, just until tender.
2. Rinse under cold water.
3. Heat one and a half tablespoons of oil in a large saucepan or wok over medium-high heat.
4. Add the shrimp, chicken or tofu, garlic and bell pepper.
5. The shrimp will cook quickly, about two minutes on each side, or until pink.
6. If using chicken, cook until just cooked through, for about five minutes, flipping only once.
7. Add a little more oil and add the beaten eggs.
8. Scramble the eggs, breaking them into small pieces with a spatula as they are cooked.
9. Add noodles, sauce, bean sprouts and peanuts to the pan.
10. Top with green onions, extra peanuts, cilantro and lime wedges.
11. Your dish is ready to be served.

❖ 3.2 Easy Thai Noodles Recipes

Cooking Time: 25 minutes

Serving Size: 3

Ingredients:
- Coleslaw mix, one bag
- Green onions, a quarter cup
- Shredded carrots, half cup
- Honey roasted peanuts, half cup
- Oil, three tbsp.
- Rotisserie chicken, two cups
- Linguini noodles, five ounces
- Cilantro, a quarter cup
- Soy sauce, one tbsp.
- Honey, five tbsp.
- Sesame oil, three tbsp.
- Red chili flakes, two tbsp.
- Minced garlic, four

Instructions:
1. While noodles are being cooked, whisk together in a small bowl the soy sauce, honey, sesame oil, garlic and red pepper flakes.

2. Pour sauce onto drained noodles, and toss together.
3. Add shredded cabbage, shredded carrots and shredded cilantro to noodle mixture and mix.
4. Then gently stir in half of the chopped cilantro, green onions and peanuts, reserving the other half for garnish.
5. Serve warm or cold and garnish with remaining cilantro, green onions and chopped peanuts.
6. Your dish is ready to be served.

❖ 3.3 Thai Red Curry Recipe

Cooking Time: 20 minutes

Serving Size: 4

Ingredients:
- Coleslaw mix, one bag
- Green onions, a quarter cup
- Thai basil, half cup
- Kefir lime leaves, half cup
- Oil, one tbsp.
- Boneless chicken thigh, eight pieces
- Coriander, for garnish
- Soy sauce, one tbsp.
- Honey, five tbsp.
- Brown sugar, half tbsp.
- Red curry paste, five tbsp.
- Minced garlic and ginger, one tsp.
- Cooked jasmine rice

Instructions:

1. Heat one tbsp. vegetable oil in a large saucepan over a medium heat and fry one tbsp. ginger and one tbsp. garlic paste.
2. Add the red curry paste, sizzle for a few secs, and then pour in the coconut milk.
3. Bring to the boil, reduce to a simmer, stir a little and wait for the oil to rise to the surface.
4. Add the skinless, boneless chicken thighs, cut into chunks, and kaffir lime leaves, and simmer for twelve mins or until the chicken is cooked through.
5. Add one tbsp. of the fish sauce and a pinch of brown sugar.
6. Bring to the boil, take off the heat and add Thai basil.
7. Spoon the curry into four bowls and top with the red chili, a thumb-sized piece of ginger and a few extra basil leaves.
8. Serve with jasmine rice.

❖ 3.4 Thai Som Tum without Papaya Recipe

Cooking Time: 15 minutes
Serving Size: 2

Ingredients:

- Lime wedges
- Unsalted cashews, two cups
- Fish sauce, two tbsp.
- Thai chili paste, one tbsp.
- Shredded carrot, one cup
- White cabbage, one cup
- Green snake beans, two cups
- Minced garlic, one tsp.
- Palm sugar, two tbsp.
- Bird's eye chili, one

Instructions:

1. In a small pan, dry roast cashews over medium high heat, tossing frequently. Roast until nuts are nearly blackened in small spots, for about four minutes.
2. Combine the lime juice, chili paste, fish sauce and sugar in a small bowl.

3. Whisk to combine evenly.
4. Using a mortar and pestle set, gently pound the garlic and bird's eye chili until both are crushed and broken into small pieces.
5. Add carrot and beans to the mortar and pound until carrots are moist and beans are crushed.
6. Add cabbage and cashews.
7. Add liquid into the bowl in bits at a time until vegetables are heavily dressed, stirring to combine.
8. Serve immediately or refrigerate and serve within a couple of hours, garnished with lime wedges.

❖ 3.5 Hot and Sour Noodle Soup with Prawns

Recipe

Cooking Time: 15 minutes

Serving Size: 4

Ingredients:
- Lime wedges
- Fish sauce, two tbsp.
- Tamarind paste, two tbsp.
- Minced garlic and ginger, one tsp.
- Glass noodles, 500g
- Water, four cups
- Tomatoes, two
- Red chili, one
- Prawns, 500g
- Snake beans, one cup
- Kaffir lime leaves, four

Instructions:

1. Place the stock, kaffir lime leaves, chili, ginger, fish sauce, tamarind paste, and water in a large heavy-based saucepan, and bring to the boil over high heat.
2. Reduce heat to medium-low and simmer for five minutes.
3. Meanwhile, place the glass noodles or vermicelli in a large heatproof bowl and pour over enough boiling water to cover.
4. Set aside for three minutes to soften, then rinse and drain well and divide among serving bowls.
5. Add the green or snake beans to the soup and simmer for a further two minutes.
6. Add the tomatoes and prawns, and then remove from the heat.
7. Stand for one minute until prawns are just cooked, then ladle soup over the noodles and garnish with coriander.
8. Your dish is ready to be served.

❖ 3.6 Thai Chicken Salad Recipe

Cooking Time: 5 minutes

Serving Size: 8

Ingredients:
- Carrots, one cup
- Cucumber, one cup
- Bok choy, two cups
- Cucumber, one cup
- Fresh mint leaves
- Green cabbage, three cups
- Chicken breast, two pounds
- Peanuts, half cup
- Olive oil, two tsp.
- Fish sauce, two tsp.
- Chili garlic sauce, two tsp.
- Honey, one tbsp.
- Peanut butter, two tbsp.
- Soy sauce, two tsp.

Instructions:
1. Whisk all the ingredients for the dressing together in a bowl or give them a shake in a mason jar.
2. You can microwave the peanut butter for fifteen seconds to soften it for easier mixing if needed.
3. Add all the salad ingredients to a large bowl along with the dressing.
4. Your dish is ready to be served.

❖ 3.7 Quick Thai Salad Recipe

Cooking Time: 5 minutes

Serving Size: 4-6

Ingredients:
- Cucumber cubes, two cups
- Bean sprouts, two cups
- Spring onion, one cup
- Shredded carrots, one cup
- Fresh mint leaves
- Fresh basil leaves
- Brown sugar, two tbsp.
- Peanuts
- Lime juice, two tsp.
- Fish sauce, two tsp.

Instructions:
1. In a bowl, mix together the vegetables and herbs.
2. Make the dressing by mixing together the fish sauce, lime juice and sugar.
3. Pour the dressing over the salad, toss to coat and scatter over the peanuts.

4. Your dish is ready to be served.

❖ 3.8 Thai Chopped Salad with Sesame Garlic Dressing Recipe

Cooking Time: 5 minutes

Serving Size: 4-6

Ingredients:
- Shredded green cabbage, two cups
- Shredded red cabbage, two cups
- Sliced red bell pepper, one cup
- Shredded carrots, one cup
- Sliced yellow bell pepper, one cup
- Shredded carrots, one cup
- Green onions, a quarter cup
- Toasted Almonds, half cup
- Honey, two tbsp.
- Cilantro, a quarter cup
- Brown sugar, two tbsp.
- Salt and pepper to taste
- Sesame oil, one tsp.
- Sesame, half cup
- Fish sauce, two tsp.
- Garlic paste, two tbsp.

Instructions:

1. Combine all of the dressing ingredients in a high-powered blender and blend until smooth and creamy.
2. Add all of the salad ingredients to a large bowl.
3. Drizzle your desired amount of the sesame garlic dressing over the salad.
4. Your dish is ready to be served.

❖ 3.9 Beef Pad Thai Recipe

Cooking Time: 15 minutes

Serving Size: 4

Ingredients:

- Chopped green onions, three
- Eggs, two
- Fresh bean sprouts, half cup
- Garlic cloves, three
- Oil, three tbsp.
- Limes, two
- Red bell pepper, one
- Flat rice noodles, eight ounces
- Dry roasted peanuts, two cups
- Soy sauce, one tbsp.
- Light brown sugar, five tbsp.
- Fish sauce, three tbsp.
- Creamy peanut butter, two tbsp.
- Rice vinegar, two tbsp.
- Siracha hot sauce, one tbsp.
- Beef strips, half pound

Instructions:

1. Place all sauce ingredients in a jar and shake until well combined.
2. Heat two tablespoon oil in a large skillet over medium-high heat.
3. Add the garlic and beef strips and cook until evenly browned on all sides and fully cooked.
4. Add the sprouts, carrots, pepper, and noodles with the beef and stir fry for one to two minutes.
5. Take the pan off the heat and mix in the sauce, green onions, and peanuts.
6. Top with cilantro and sesame seeds.
7. Your dish is ready to be served.

❖ 3.10 Pork Pad Thai Recipe

Cooking Time: 15 minutes

Serving Size: 4

Ingredients:
- Chopped green onions, three
- Eggs, two
- Fresh bean sprouts, half cup
- Garlic cloves, three
- Oil, three tbsp.
- Limes, two
- Red bell pepper, one
- Flat rice noodles, eight ounces
- Dry roasted peanuts, two cups
- Soy sauce, one tbsp.
- Light brown sugar, five tbsp.
- Fish sauce, three tbsp.
- Creamy peanut butter, two tbsp.
- Rice vinegar, two tbsp.
- Siracha hot sauce, one tbsp.
- Pork strips, half pound

Instructions:
1. Place all sauce ingredients in a jar and shake until well combined.
2. Heat two tablespoon oil in a large skillet over medium-high heat.
3. Add the garlic and pork strips and cook until evenly browned on all sides and fully cooked.
4. Add the sprouts, carrots, pepper, and noodles in with the pork and stir fry for one to two minutes.
5. Take the pan off the heat and mix in the sauce, green onions, and peanuts.
6. Top with cilantro and sesame seeds.

❖ 3.11 Thai Fish Curry Recipe

Cooking Time: 30 minutes
Serving Size: 4

Ingredients:
- Coconut cream, two cups
- Coconut milk, one cup
- Barracuda fish, 800 g
- Salt, to taste
- Kaffir lime leaves, twenty
- Lemongrass, two stalks
- Turmeric, one tsp.
- Thai dry chilies, two
- Black pepper, one tsp.
- Shrimp paste, two tbsp.
- Lime wedges, 4
- Crushed red chili flakes, two tsp.
- Bean sprouts
- Lemon basil
- Chinese long beans
- Fresh rice noodles, two pounds
- Minced garlic, two tbsp.

- Deep fried chilies

Instructions:
1. Bring a pot of water to boil, and then boil the fish for about ten minutes until fully cooked.
2. Once the fish is cool, carefully take off the skin and debone all the meat.
3. Cut the turmeric into small pieces as well.
4. Then add the lemongrass, turmeric, garlic, and peppercorns, and pound for about thirty minutes until a relatively smooth paste.
5. In a large pot or sauce pan, add all the coconut milk and curry paste, then turn on medium heat.
6. Stir gently, and only in one direction, making sure all the curry paste dissolves into the coconut milk.
7. Add the minced fish, season with salt, and tear the kaffir lime leaves in half and add them to the curry.
8. Your dish is ready to be served.

❖ 3.12 Thai Basil Chicken Recipe

Cooking Time: 20 minutes
Serving Size: 6

Ingredients:
- Fresh Thai basil leaves, two cups
- Oyster sauce, two tsp.
- Honey, two tbsp.
- Boneless chicken, two pounds
- Brown sugar, two tbsp.
- Salt and pepper to taste
- Canola oil, one tsp.
- Lime juice, two tbsp.
- Lime wedges, 4
- Crushed red chili flakes, two tsp.
- Fish sauce, two tsp.
- Minced garlic, two tbsp.

Instructions:
1. In a large bowl, stir together sliced chicken, oyster sauce, soy sauce, fish sauce, lime juice and brown sugar until evenly coated.

2. Allow chicken to marinate while preparing the rest of the meal.
3. Heat canola oil in a large skillet or wok over medium-high heat.
4. Add garlic and red pepper flakes and sauté until fragrant, about thirty seconds.
5. Cook, stirring frequently, until chicken is cooked through and no longer pink, about five minutes.
6. Add basil leaves and continue to cook.
7. Your dish is ready to be served.

❖ 3.13 Thai Crunch Salad with Peanut Butter Dressing Recipe

Cooking Time: 5 minutes
Serving Size: 4-6

Ingredients:
- Shredded green cabbage, two cups
- Shredded red cabbage, two cups
- Sliced red bell pepper, one cup
- Shredded carrots, one cup
- Sliced yellow bell pepper, one cup
- Shredded carrots, one cup
- Green onions, a quarter cup
- Toasted Almonds, half cup
- Honey, two tbsp.
- Cilantro, a quarter cup
- Brown sugar, two tbsp.
- Salt and pepper to taste
- Sesame oil, one tsp.
- Peanut butter, half cup
- Fish sauce, two tsp.
- Lime juice, two tbsp.

Instructions:

1. Combine all of the dressing ingredients in a high-powered blender.
2. Add all of the salad ingredients to a large bowl.
3. Drizzle your desired amount of the peanut dressing over the salad.
4. Your dish is ready to be served.

❖ 3.14 Thai Chicken Coconut Curry Recipe

Cooking Time: 25 minutes
Serving Size: 6

Ingredients:
- Yellow onion, one
- Ground coriander, one tbsp.
- Soy sauce, a quarter cup
- Fish sauce, one tbsp.
- Coconut milk, one cup
- Shredded carrots, one cup
- Garlic and ginger paste, one tbsp.
- Oil, two tbsp.
- Fresh spinach leaves, three cups
- Cilantro, a quarter cup
- Brown sugar, two tbsp.
- Salt and pepper to taste
- Thai red curry paste, three tbsp.
- Chicken breast, one pound
- Rice to serve
- Lime juice, two tbsp.

Instructions:

1. To a large skillet, add the oil, onion, and sauté over medium-high heat until the onion begins to soften.
2. Add the chicken and cook for about five minutes.
3. Add the garlic, ginger, coriander, and cook.
4. Add the coconut milk, carrots, Thai curry paste, salt, pepper, and stir to combine.
5. Reduce the heat to medium, and allow mixture to gently boil.
6. Add the spinach, lime juice, and stir to combine.
7. Taste and optionally add brown sugar.
8. Evenly sprinkle with the cilantro.

❖ 3.15 Thai Green Curry Soup Recipe

Cooking Time: 20 minutes
Serving Size: 4

Ingredients:
- Sliced mushrooms, one cup
- Vegetable stock, four cups
- Broccoli florets, three cups
- Coconut milk, a quarter cup
- Brown sugar, one tbsp.
- Soy sauce, one tsp.
- Thai green curry paste, two tbsp.
- Sesame oil, two tbsp.
- Salt to taste
- Crushed peanuts, one tbsp.
- Spring onion greens, one tbsp.
- Rice noodles, half pound
- Fresh basil, half cup
- Lime, two
- Minced garlic, one tsp.

Instructions:

1. Add the vegetables together and stir fry them over high heat for five minutes.
2. In the same saucepan, add the garlic, ginger, and green curry paste.
3. Sauté the curry paste for few minutes to combine it evenly with the oil.
4. Add the coconut milk, brown sugar, and soy sauce.
5. Next, add the vegetable stock, salt, and stir to combine.
6. Taste and add more coconut milk for a milder taste or green chilies to make it spicy.
7. Add the vermicelli noodles.
8. Once noodles are cooked, add stir fry vegetables and give the soup a good stir.
9. Just before serving, garnish soup with fresh herbs, crushed peanuts, and juice of lemon.

❖ 3.16 Thai Rice Noodles with Chicken and Asparagus Recipe

Cooking Time: 40 minutes

Serving Size: 4

Ingredients:
- Asparagus, half pound
- Brown sugar, one tbsp.
- Soy sauce, a quarter cup
- Fish sauce, one tbsp.
- Chili garlic sauce, one tbsp.
- Oil, two tbsp.
- Chicken breast, eight ounces
- Rice noodles, half pound
- Minced garlic, one tsp.

Instructions:
1. Heat oil in large skillet over medium-high heat.
2. Add garlic and stir fry until golden.
3. Add fish sauce or salt and chicken.
4. Add soy sauce, chili pepper sauce, and brown sugar.
5. Mix until sugar is dissolved.

6. Drain noodles and add to skillet along with asparagus.
7. Your dish is ready to be served.

❖ 3.17 Thai Chicken Fried Rice Recipe

Cooking Time: 30 minutes

Serving Size: 4

Ingredients:
- Fish sauce, two tbsp.
- Egg, one
- Soy sauce, half cup
- Cooked brown jasmine rice, three cups
- Tomatoes, two
- Cilantro, half cup
- Salt and pepper, to taste
- Vegetable oil, two tbsp.
- Thai chili peppers, three
- Toasted walnuts, half cup
- Chicken breast, eight ounces
- Onion, one
- Scallions, half cup
- Minced garlic, one tsp.

Instructions:
1. Season chicken lightly with salt and pepper.

2. When the oil is hot, add the chicken and cook on high until it is browned all over and cooked through.
3. Remove chicken from wok and set aside, add the eggs, pinch of salt and cook a minute or two until done.
4. Add the remaining oil to the wok and add the onion, scallions and garlic.
5. Sauté for a minute, add the chili pepper if using, tomatoes and stir in all the rice.
6. Add the soy sauce and fish sauce stir to mix all the ingredients.
7. Adjust soy sauce if needed.
8. Your dish is ready to be served.

Chapter 4: Thai Dinner Recipes

This Chapter contains those easy Thai dinner recipes that you have been longing to make in your kitchen.

❖ 4.1 Thai Slow Cooker Chicken Curry Recipe

Cooking Time: 3 hours
Serving Size: 4

Ingredients:

- Salt, a pinch
- Chicken breast pieces, two pounds
- Coconut milk, one cup
- Cilantro, one cup
- Vegetable oil, two tbsp.
- Water, 500ml
- Crushed red pepper, one tbsp.
- Minced garlic, half tsp.
- Curry powder, two tsp.
- Brown or jasmine rice, two cups

Instructions:

1. Whisk together the coconut milk, curry powder, salt, crushed red pepper and garlic in a slow cooker.
2. Add the remaining ingredients and cook on high for three hours.
3. Your dish is ready to be served with brown rice or jasmine rice.

❖ 4.2 Thai Slow Cooker Whole Cauliflower Curry Recipe

Cooking Time: 3 hours
Serving Size: 4

Ingredients:
- Salt, a pinch
- Coconut milk, one cup
- Cilantro, one cup
- Cauliflower, one whole
- Vegetable oil, two tbsp.
- Water, 500ml
- Crushed red pepper, one tbsp.
- Minced garlic, half tsp.
- Curry powder, two tsp.
- Quinoa, two cups

Instructions:
1. Whisk together the coconut milk, curry powder, salt, crushed red pepper and garlic in a slow cooker.
2. Add the remaining ingredients and cook on high for three hours.

3. Your dish is ready to be served with any rice of your choice.

❖ 4.3 Thai Slow Cooker Chicken Carrot Potato Soup Recipe

Cooking Time: 3 hours
Serving Size: 4

Ingredients:
- Potato, three cups
- Garlic cloves, four
- Water, four cups
- Carrots, three cups
- Chicken, two pounds
- Coriander seeds, two teaspoons
- Chopped coriander, a handful
- Hot paprika, two tsp.
- Grated lemon zest, two
- Kaffir lime leaves, four
- Coconut milk, one cup

Instructions:
1. Mix all the ingredients together and cover it to simmer for three hours.
2. Your soup is ready to be served.

❖ 4.4 Thai Slow Cooker Coconut Quinoa Curry Recipe

Cooking Time: 3 hours

Serving Size: 4

Ingredients:
- Salt, a pinch
- Coconut milk, one cup
- Cilantro, one cup
- Vegetable oil, two tbsp.
- Water, 500ml
- Crushed red pepper, one tbsp.
- Minced garlic, half tsp.
- Curry powder, two tsp.
- Quinoa, two cups

Instructions:
1. Whisk together the coconut milk, curry powder, salt, crushed red pepper and garlic in a slow cooker.
2. Add the remaining ingredients and cook on high for three hours.
3. Your dish is ready to be served.

❖ 4.5 Thai Slow Cooker Eggplant Curry

Recipe

Cooking Time: 3 hours

Serving Size: 4

Ingredients:

- Salt, a pinch
- Eggplant, two cups
- Coconut milk, one cup
- Cilantro, one cup
- Vegetable oil, two tbsp.
- Water, 500ml
- Crushed red pepper, one tbsp.
- Minced garlic, half tsp.
- Curry powder, two tsp.
- Brown or jasmine rice, two cups

Instructions:

1. Whisk together the coconut milk, curry powder, salt, crushed red pepper and garlic in a slow cooker.
2. Add the remaining ingredients and cook on high for three hours.

3. Your dish is ready to be served with brown rice or jasmine rice.

❖ 4.6 Thai Slow Cooker Yellow Curry Recipe

Cooking Time: 2 hours

Serving Size: 4

Ingredients:
- Salt, a pinch
- Chickpeas, two cups
- Coconut milk, one cup
- Butternut squash, one
- Vegetable oil, two tbsp.
- Water, 500ml
- Carrots, two cups
- Brown rice, four cups

Instructions:
1. Tip in the chickpeas, butternut squash and carrots. Then stir through the coconut milk along with 500ml water.
2. Season and stir through half of the coriander.
3. Spoon the curry into deep bowls, scatter with the remaining coriander.
4. Serve with rice and lime wedges for squeezing over.

❖ 4.7 Thai Slow Cooker Vegetable Massaman Curry Recipe

Cooking Time: 3 hours

Serving Size: 6

Ingredients:

- Quinoa, two cups
- Coconut milk, half cup
- Vegetable broth, half cup
- Tomatoes, half cup
- Brown sugar, one tsp.
- Tamari sauce, one tbsp.
- Cauliflower, one
- Potato, one cup
- Green beans, one cup
- Salt and pepper, to taste
- Siracha hot sauce, one tsp.
- Peanut butter, half cup
- Peanuts, half cup

Instructions:

1. Stir in the broth, tomatoes, fish sauce, tamari and brown sugar.
2. Add the cauliflower and potatoes, and toss to coat. Cover and cook until the vegetables are tender.
3. Combine the coconut milk and peanut butter in a heatproof bowl and microwave until warm.
4. Pour the coconut milk mixture into the slow cooker, and add the green beans and peanuts. Cover and cook until warmed through.
5. Add the sriracha, and season with salt and pepper.
6. Serve the curry over rice or quinoa, and sprinkle with chopped peanuts and cilantro.

❖ 4.8 Thai Pumpkin and Veggie Curry Recipe

Cooking Time: 40 minutes

Serving Size: 4

Ingredients:

- Corn, half cup
- Red bell pepper, two
- Pumpkin, two
- Salt, a pinch
- Coconut milk, one cup
- Thai red curry paste, four tbsp.
- Vegetable oil, two tbsp.
- Chili, one tsp.
- Butternut squash, two cups
- Water, 200ml
- Shallots, half cup
- Brown rice, four cups

Instructions:

1. Add the shallots with a pinch of salt and fry for ten mins over a medium heat until softened.

2. Add the curry paste and chili to the dish and fry for two mins.
3. Tip in the pumpkin, vegetables, and then stir through the coconut milk along with 200ml water.
4. Season and stir through half of the coriander and corn.
5. Spoon the curry into deep bowls, scatter with the remaining coriander and serve with rice and lime wedges for squeezing over.

❖ 4.9 Thai Vegan Drunken Noodles Recipe

Cooking Time: 15 minutes

Serving Size: 2

Ingredients:
- Green onion, one
- Bell pepper, one
- Thai basil, a handful
- Garlic and ginger paste, one tsp.
- Sesame oil, two tbsp.
- Soy sauce, one tsp.
- Oyster sauce, one tsp.
- Fish sauce, one tsp.
- Salt and black pepper, to taste
- Red Thai chili, one
- Shallots, half cup

Instructions:
1. Cook the vegetables in the sesame oil.
2. Add spices and sauces into the mixture and then add the noodles and mix thoroughly.
3. Your dish is ready to be served.

❖ 4.10 Thai Tofu Green Curry with Quinoa Recipe

Cooking Time: 40 minutes

Serving Size: 4

Ingredients:

- Quinoa, four cups
- Salt, a pinch
- Coconut milk, one cup
- Thai green curry paste, four tbsp.
- Vegetable oil, two tbsp.
- Chili, one tsp.
- Tofu, two cups
- Water, 200ml
- Shallots, half cup

Instructions:

1. Add the shallots with a pinch of salt and fry for ten mins over a medium heat until softened and beginning to caramelize.
2. Add the curry paste and chili to the dish and fry for two mins.

3. Tip in the tofu, and then stir through the coconut milk along with 200ml water.
4. Season and stir through half of the coriander and corn.
5. Spoon the curry into deep bowls, scatter with the remaining coriander and serve with cooked quinoa and lime wedges for squeezing over.

Conclusion

While living a busy life, food becomes the source of happiness for individuals in the 21st century. Different cuisines are available in the world and each of them being totally different from the other. Thai cuisine covers dishes from Thailand and Thai foods are extremely popular in whole world.

Thai cuisine is one of the most loved and appreciated cuisines in the world. This book is all about making Thai cooking as easy as possible for you. In this book, there are 77 different recipes covering the breakfast, lunch, dinner and snack sections of your day. You can learn Thai cooking at home now with this amazing cookbook. With the detailed ingredient and instruction section your Thai cooking will be your family's top most favorite in the world.

Ingram Content Group UK Ltd.
Milton Keynes UK
UKHW020626210623
423802UK00010B/29